The Groundwork of Eugenics

Karl Pearson

BIBLIOLIFE

THE GROUNDWORK OF EUGENICS

by

KARL PEARSON, F.R.S.

"You ask whether I shall discuss 'man.' I think I shall avoid the subject, as so surrounded with prejudices; though I fully admit it is the highest and most interesting problem for the naturalist."

Letter of Darwin to Wallace 1857

SECOND EDITION

LONDON

Published by the Cambridge University Press, Fetter Lane, E.C. 4

1912

PREFATORY NOTE

THIS paper gives the substance of two lectures
delivered as an introduction to a Course on the Science of
National Eugenics at the Galton Laboratory, February 23
and March 2, 1909.

It is published because the Staff of that Laboratory has
found the need of some introduction to the science of
Eugenics, which shall place the results of their investigations in a simple form before the layman.   The aim of the
present series of publications is to state the conclusions
drawn from laborious statistical investigations and their
bearing on national welfare in non-technical language suited
to the general reader.

THE GROUNDWORK OF EUGENICS

DOES a real biological science of the evolution of human societies exist? This is the problem foremost in the minds of many thinkers to-day, and likely in the near future to force itself irresistibly on the attention not only of statesmen, but of all who have the national welfare at heart.

Can we place ourselves outside the community of which we form a part, and study the effects upon it of environment, of occupation, of nourishment and of breeding in the same judicial manner as the owner of a herd of shorthorns approaches the like problems? The question cannot be answered with a light 'Yes' or 'No' according to the taste or sentiment of the respondent. We are not in the position of the owner, but we are members of the herd ourselves— with all the feelings of our class, the prejudices of our education or want of education, the strong emotions of our sex, and the complex passions of our race and stock We cannot make direct experiments on our fellow-men, and study training and nurture and parentage as it is possible for the owner of a thoroughbred stud to do. Yet if these admitted difficulties forced us to answer 'No' to our question, they would equally compel us to deny the possibility of a real study of medicine. The clinical ward, the post-mortem room, the pathological laboratory, the asylum and the sanatorium— nay, the bared soul as well as the bared body of many a private patient—compel the higher type of medical man, who is ever student as well as adviser, to repress sternly the personal and place himself outside the herd for the furtherance of his science and the effectiveness of his craft.

To him also social conditions render direct experiment largely impracticable. He can only seek for and may possibly discover a group of his fellows, who are making the required experiment on their own initiative. But such is the great variety of human conduct and taste, such the extent of human blindness and folly, that it is possible with time and energy to discover and observe groups of individuals making most of the experiments, which the student of medicine or eugenics might wish to institute had he the aloofness of a superman controlling a herd of men

Man himself makes the experiments which are directly impossible for the eugenist This stock marries kin for six generations; those parents surfeit themselves with alcohol; there the tuberculous taint meets insanity ; here the man of genius marries into his class ; there he takes a woman of the people There is hardly a phase of nurture and of environment, or of parentage and of ancestry which cannot be followed up,—not in a single experiment, but in repeated experiments,—if the time and energy to investigate are forthcoming.

The science of eugenics does not propose to experiment on man; it endeavours to lay before us the results of man's experiments on himself, and this in such numerous cases that the evidence must carry with it conviction. Our object is to form an analytical record of man's experiments on himself, to draw from the history of his successes and failures the biological laws which govern his social development, and upon the basis of the knowledge thus gained to predict what lines of conduct foster, what lines check national welfare. Conduct may be enforced by a social or by a legal sanction. The possibilities of enforcing conduct by such sanctions form the subject of ‘Practical Eugenics,’ which I shall exclude entirely from consideration in this lecture.

It can only be properly discussed after we have measured the present state of our knowledge, and are able to estimate its relation to our existing social organisation. Before discussing practical eugenics we must know the relative weight of nature and nurture, of heredity and race, of environment and training. These are wide subjects, on which at present —even if we confine our attention to man—we have only partial knowledge. Some phases of what we do know will be discussed in the later lectures, and when these are concluded we can return with greater fitness to what is feasible in practical eugenics

Meanwhile I return to my point that, while the student of eugenics can make no direct experiments on man, he can observe those experiments which mankind is every day on so vast a scale making upon itself. And he has to observe those experiments in the calm scientific manner of the physician in his clinic; he must not be led away to immediate action by the first individual case, which appeals to his sympathy and emotions. The general rule can only be learnt when the statistics of many individual cases have been dealt with. Each characteristic, each virtue and each vice is protean in its forms, and not until we have massed case upon case in our experience can we deduce the general drift of the whole series.

I would illustrate this by an attempt to consider some of the sources of feeble-mindedness in the children of the industrial classes made to my knowledge quite recently in a large manufacturing town. The family history of several hundred mentally defective children was followed up with considerable energy and success. The result was that a most striking amount of alcoholism was demonstrated to exist in the ancestry, and it was supposed that this investigation confirmed the view that alcoholism in the parent was one of the chief sources of mental defect in children. I suggested that a control series of normal children from the same school districts should also have their family histories worked out; this was a harder task as the parents naturally resented inquiry, but the result showed a 'striking amount of alcoholism' in the parents of the normal children ! It would have taken far larger and more detailed data to determine whether the intensity of alcoholism was greater in the ancestry of the mentally defective or in that of the normal children. My informant—a very keen and active social worker—adopted the view that the prevalent alcoholism showed that the *whole* industrial population of the district was degenerate, and that it was purely the result of chance that some families had and some had not produced mentally defective children. All that had been done was to divide the population into two groups by the presence or absence of children of this character.

Now personally I might not be prepared to accept this view, I might argue that alcoholism is a sign, just as much as feeble-mindedness, of mental abnormality and not the cause of the latter. But the important point I want to emphasise at present is : that we are not compelled because we find alcoholic parents to the feeble-minded to assume that alcohol is the source of feeble-mindedness. It is a very complex statistical problem to determine whether alcoholism is more or less prevalent in the parents of one or other class of children. And had it been determined as more prevalent, it would not follow that alcoholism was the source of the feeble-mindedness ; both may be different manifestations of the same ancestral weakness. You will find this a useful point to bear in mind, when you note how alcoholism occurs in association with insane, feeble-minded, deaf-mute, criminal and generally defective stocks. But association is not necessarily causation, and we may waste on the fight against alcohol energy which could only destroy the admitted social evils, if it were directed to the extermination of the degenerate stocks themselves.

I have dwelt somewhat at length on this problem of feeble-mindedness in children and alcoholism in ancestry because it is not only a typical case, but a nationally important case. It is such an easy stage to pass from the inspection of a few individual instances to a state of intense social feeling—to the demand for the use of the axe in the beer saloon—that we want above all things some calm scientific investigation of human society and its biological growth removed from the cries of the market-place and the appeals of political parties. It is on this ground that the study of human society must, I claim, be admitted to an adequate place in the curriculum of our universities It is not so many years ago since the professor of animal biology and the biological laboratory were unknown to the academic world. Think what that absence meant for the knowledge of living forms—nay, for the general culture of mankind, for it marks a date before Charles Darwin had revolutionised our outlook on life! Are we to assert that this great biological movement, which has won its way to equal rights in the academic fraternity, is to stop short when it approaches the subject of man as a gregarious animal? Is there no science of those vital factors which may improve or impair, physically or mentally, the racial qualities of future generations? And if there be such a science is it not the first duty of the universities to discover and propound its laws?

Now the genuine man of science will never admit that any portion of nature, that any group of mental or physical phenomena is *anomic*, or without definite and discoverable sequences. We do not despair of meteorology because the method and the man that will make it a fairly precise science is yet in the seeking. Astronomy sprang triumphant from astrology, and the great Kepler himself, son of a woman tried for witchcraft, started life by writing horoscopes. It would be as reasonable to throw alchemy and Paracelsus in the balance against modern chemical science, as to assert that we must measure the possibilities of a study of human society to-day by the sociology of yesterday and the social science of the day before.

The difference is great and it is threefold. In the first place it is a difference of mental training and intellectual attitude. It is the difference between the student of humanities and the student of science. Take a text-book of political economy such as is put into the hands of every student, for example that of President Walker ; there is not a single numerical association worked out, the very numerical tables given are purely hypothetical constructions of the author introduced to illustrate the logomachy ; the whole reasoning is a reasoning about verbal notions, where we demand a determination of the correlation of associated causes based upon recorded experience. Social science followed the earlier political economy, and provided verbose discussion, where the first need was well-selected and well-recorded observation. The fundamental change in our attitude is from that of the essay writer to that of the scientific inquirer. Let me illustrate my point by a concrete example I take the influence of the unhealthy trade of the father and the factory occupation of the mother on the health and intelligence of the children Well, very much has been talked, very much has been written, on that subject ; but the only real way to answer the problem is by examining statistically the effect on some 20,000 or 30,000 children of the occupations of their parents. This is precisely what Miss Elderton has recently done, and I do not believe that any verbal discussion on what ought to follow can be anything like as satisfactory as noting what actually has happened. The next point is that even when a few generations ago statistics were collected and exhibited, there was no effective method of deducing the kernel from them   Our power of interpreting statistics, of measuring the exact degree of relationship between associated phenomena, has enormously increased during the last few decades   We have really to deal with the discovery of a new calculus, which means not only for social problems, but in many other fields, a very potent instrument for analysing numerical records   The association of phenomena, the interrelationship of quality and environment, the dependence of characters on nurture and on nature can now be measured with an ease and accuracy which were practically unknown twenty years ago

When we come to deal with man in the mass, to estimate the characters of each group of the social body, to weigh the amounts of virtue and of vice, of health and disease, of intelligence and mental defect, it is not of the individual but of the assemblage or array with certain qualities that we have to treat.   This array may consist of several hundreds or thousands, and its common or 'recognition' marks, be they social or anti-social, its fertility, its dominance or decay must form the subject of our study.

If you consider that point for a moment, namely, that we propose to study the differentiated groups of mankind within the same social body, to ascertain which of these differentiated groups is, owing to its characteristics, the most effective for this or that purpose, to determine not only its rate of increase, but the extent to which its qualities are transmitted to its offspring and modified by environment, then you will perceive that what we are concerned with in the main is the *actuarial* treatment of large numbers You will understand why great statistical advances had to be made, before it became possible in an effective and not merely periphrastic manner to study those agencies which may improve or impair the racial qualities of future generations, in a word, to study eugenics We may have to collect our data from individual cases, but our results apply to the differentiated group as a whole. In this sense the science of eugenics is not personal—practical eugenics may touch personal conduct—but the generalisations of the science apply as I have endeavoured to indicate to groups of many individuals, differentiated by this or that series of characters, and subject to this or that nurture or environment.

This transition from declamatory assertion to statistical proof is the characteristic feature of eugenics And I need to insist on it *here*. It is not many weeks ago[1] since the folly of the Eugenics Laboratory was held up to the students of this College because it was asserted to lay much stress on nature and little on nurture, to emphasise heredity and neglect environment. I have heard elementary teachers assert that we were depriving them of their *raison d'être*, which they told us was the conversion of bad material into good by a fitting environment, by a judicious course of training and nurture. Far be it from me to underrate without study the effects of environment ; I hold no brief against environment ; I am not pledged to any formula of nature against nurture. But I am unable to find that our declamatory friends have themselves made any quantitative study of the relative value of nature and nurture, and while they proclaimed our folly downstairs, there was comfortably lodged

---

[1] February, 1909.

in the pigeon-holes in the Laboratory upstairs a good deal
of evidence as to the relative intensity of the inheritance
and the environment factors. I refer to this point as an
illustration of what I mean, when I say that the method of
investigating the laws of human societies is changing from
the verbal to the statistical, and the problem of the parts
played by nature and nurture cannot be solved by appealing
vaguely to the excellent work of the schoolmaster or to the
admitted advantages of Peabody Buildings.

As we are here on the site of what is not unlikely to prove
one of the great battlefields of eugenics, I would illustrate,
by one example only, how the problem of nature *versus*
nurture has been prejudged. There is hardly a practical
text-book on ophthalmology which does not accept the
theory that the school is the hotbed for the production of
short-sight. If you endeavour to trace this traditional attitude
to its source, you will find that the main authority for it is
the work of a German ophthalmologist, Cohn, who examined
the eyes of several thousand children, and recorded their
increasing myopia with increased number of years at school.
From this it is easy, but not logical, to assert that years of
school life produce myopia. It would be equally valid to
assert that the number of years a boy spends on arithmetic
lengthen his head, or, perhaps, more valid still to say that
the lengthening of his head produces myopia. Unfortun-
ately modern civilisation does not admit of our studying
several thousand children of civilised parents with normal
home environment, growing up without school, and ascer-
taining whether their short-sight would or would not
increase with growth

But Cohn's original work gives us ground for pause ; he
has not only published a table giving the years at school,
but also a table giving the years of age in conjunction with

short-sight, and thence flow by modern statistical methods
two definite facts :—

(i) That myopia is more closely connected with years of
life than with the number of years at school.

(ii) That allowing for the high correlation between years
of life and years at school, then for a constant age there
is sensibly no relation between the intensity of short-
sightedness and the length of school life.

Myopia is thus quite sensibly related to age, but if age be
a measure of some continued and detrimental environment,
that environment does not appear to be school life.

I cite this widely accepted theory—that school is the
hotbed for the production of short-sightedness—as an
excellent illustration of the old and the new methods.

Miss Barrington, who has recently[1] been investigating this
special subject of vision, has endeavoured to find some feature
of home environment—the overcrowding, or the economic,
moral and physical surroundings of home and parentage—
which may be definitely associated with defective sight.
She fails to discover any substantial influence at all—the
intensity of environmental influence is insignificant as compared with the strength we can demonstrate to exist in this
case for the factor of inheritance.

As I have said I hold no brief for nature against nurture,
but I do demand that their relative intensity shall be
measured, not theorised about. There will in the future be
big battles on this field of nurture and nature; I would ask
those of you who hold the lists to see that the combatants
shall fight not with opinions and words, but with facts, and,
what is more, properly interpreted facts.

Let us pass from the spirit and method of eugenics to
the third cause which has made it possible for a real study

[1] February, 1909.

of the laws of human society to be evolved now. That cause is the great progress in the knowledge of heredity which has been made by biology in recent years. With the main features of that knowledge most of you are probably familiar, but there are certain fundamental points of it which bear so closely on the science of eugenics, that we must linger briefly over them. Foremost among these is the far-reaching distinction between the somatic and germ cells of an individual By aid of the latter and the latter only, can, at least in the higher forms of life, a new individual start, and directly from the germ cells of the parent arise in the first place the germ cells of the new life. This hypothesis of the continuity of the germ plasma has been fundamental as a biological conception since it was propounded by Weismann, and its important bearing on eugenics is manifest; it does not involve but it is closely allied to the principle of the non-inheritance of acquired characters. Darwin thought it desirable to invent a vast system of particles which pass from each body-cell and carry its characters to the germ cells of the parent, whence they are transmitted to the offspring. The actual manner of passage from somatic to germ cell, whether by blood or nerve, has never been settled, the 'pangene' has never been corporeally located. In the more modern view the bodily resemblance of parent and offspring arises, not because the somatic cells of the one have contributed to the somatic cells of the other, but because both are the product in the moiety of a continuous germ plasm. There is not the least doubt that this explanation is simpler and more consonant with our present knowledge. But once accepted, we see :—

(i) That the possibility of transmitting an acquired character depends on the somatic cells being able to affect the germ cells.

(ii) That the effect on the germ cells must be to produce a character similar to that acquired by the original somatic cells in a second somatic product.

Now there is no logical reason for *a priori* denying that some modifications of the somatic cells may disturb the equilibrium of the germ cells. The continuity of the germ plasm is not equivalent to its uniqueness. The slightest examination of a human family shows that all the germ cells of one individual cannot be alike, the germ plasm contains many possibilities. It is conceivable that modifying the somatic cells as by excessive under- or over-nourishment, some of these germ possibilities may be rendered less probable or even eliminated—age might achieve the same end. But without something corresponding to Darwin's 'pangenes' it is inconceivable that change in the somatic cells could produce an allied possibility in the same direction in the germ cells.

The improbability of the somatic cells discharging material character-bearers to be reabsorbed by the germ cells is physiologically great, but it might have to be faced, if there were any good evidence for the inheritance of acquired characters. The evidence for this may be classed as follows :—

(*a*) If acquired characters were inherited evolution would have proceeded at a much greater rate. The reply to this is that in the light of recent physical work there is no need to quicken up evolution ; we now know that the biologists and geologists were right and the physicists and mathematicians wrong in the length they fixed for the life of the earth. Further, if acquired characters were inherited, they would certainly have involved the inheritance of acquired degeneracy and defect as well as of acquired advantage, and this would not have worked wholly for progression.

(*b*) Direct experiments[1].

(i) The most famous are those of Brown-Séquard, who is usually asserted to have produced epilepsy artificially in guinea-pigs, and found it inherited in the offspring. The actual experiments are by no means of this decisive character. The injured animals had among their young nineteen who suffered from some defect of their nervous system, and merely two out of these nineteen had a disease which might be termed epilepsy. Westphal undertook twelve years later a similar set of experiments and found *one* case in which the two offspring of an epileptic pair were epileptic. Obersteiner in 1875 found in thirty-two young two cases in which he believed the artificial epilepsy of the parents to be found again in the offspring. In the fifteen following years he failed to repeat the experiment, because he could not artificially create the epilepsy, which suggests that the first material may have belonged to an epileptic stock. Sommer in trying again to repeat such experiments came only to negative results. It will be seen that the Brown-Séquard experiments are wholly inconclusive and must remain so.

(ii) A second section of experimental work is that on acquired immunity. Very small doses of poison gradually administered produce an immunity against large doses. It has been found that this immunity is transmitted to the offspring and the offspring are for a limited time immune to the poison. Important experiments of Ehrlich have been claimed as evidence of the inheritance of acquired characters. But there is a striking exception to the rule, *immunity of the father produces no effect on the offspring*. It is only the immunity of the mother which influences the offspring. The view that the immunity is produced by 'antibodies' in the

---

[1] We are only concerned with those on mammals. In the case of plants and insects there is at present much controversy and little firm ground.

serum of the blood, depends upon other results as to immunity, but it suffices to explain without any inheritance of acquired characters how the mother transmits to unborn offspring immunity, as she is well known to be able to transmit disease.

A direct experiment on a large scale is that of vaccination, which, continued for many generations, has not produced permanent immunity from small-pox in the race. Precisely the same result occurs with diphtheria immunity. Werniche has shown that an immune mother, but *not an immune* father, will produce immune children. The immunity thus acquired may last as long as three months, but it disappears with the grandchildren.

It would be as reasonable to speak of these cases as the 'inheritance' of acquired characters, as it would be to speak of a newly vaccinated baby 'inheriting' from the calf an immunity from small-pox.

(iii) Actual experiments have been made on mutilation-inheritance. In 1887 Zacharias, at the gathering of German Naturalists, appeared with two tailless kittens, the offspring of a mother who had been curtailed. But the pedigree of father and mother for many generations would have to be carefully scanned in order that we might be clear as to ancestry, and cats are not infrequently born tailless without a tailless family history. Weismann in twenty-two successive generations of curtailed mice had 1592 tailed offspring and none born in any degree tailless, and Bos and Von Rosenthal have confirmed on both rats and mice these experiments[1].

That unhealthy life, alcohol, excess of any kind, may cause weakened somatic cells to react on the germ cells, and affect the physique of the offspring, may be accepted, but this does

---

[1] Martius (*Pathogenese innerer Krankheiten*, 1909) gives a trenchant criticism of all this evidence to which I am much indebted.

not involve the inheritance of acquired characters. Indeed the whole of the proofs recently given that drunkenness is found in the parents of idiots, epileptics, the insane and the criminal, and of women who cannot suckle their own off-spring, fail because they do not satisfactorily demonstrate that the drunkenness was acquired by a normal stock, in which no degeneracy was known before the parent took to drink. If we start, not from the offspring of the alcoholic, but from the alcoholic themselves, and work *backwards*, we find in the majority of cases that they come of alcoholic, epileptic or degenerate stocks. Hence while we are not forced to deny that injured somatic cells *may* sometimes degrade the germ cells, we must be very stringent in our criticism of the type of proof habitually given of such interaction. It would indeed seem that while Nature had made it easy for an individual to modify his bodily cells, she has made it very hard for the toxine in either blood or lymph to reach the germ cells. As Martius puts it. 'The individual stands in far greater danger than the race.'

It may not be out of place at this point to remind you of the experiments by which Mr Galton endeavoured to test Darwin's theory of pangenesis. He interchanged the blood of two types of rabbits, but found absolutely no change in the character of the offspring procreated after the inter-change. This is strong, if not wholly conclusive, evidence that no 'pangenes' are carried by the blood

(c) Lastly we have a great deal of loose and illusory argument, which centres round the name of Herbert Spencer, and which is not uncommonly used by educationalists, when trying—which is quite unnecessary—to justify their work to their fellow-men There is a very apt tale about Herbert Spencer, told by Mr Galton in his 'Memories' Herbert Spencer once said in the presence of Huxley and others :

'You fellows would little think that I wrote a tragedy when I was young.' Huxley said promptly. 'I know what it was about' Spencer declared it was impossible as he had never shown or even spoken of it to any one before. Huxley persisted. Spencer put him to the test Huxley replied: 'It was the history of a beautiful induction killed by a nasty little fact.'

The beautiful induction, that human progress has been accelerated by the acquired results of education inherited by the offspring, is killed by the nasty little fact, that no conclusive experiment on mammals which showed definite action of somatic cells upon germ cells *in an attuned* direction has ever been made, and from the standpoint of modern biology such action is not only nigh unthinkable, but must be as largely harmful as useful. The race has evolved protection for itself from individual excess, by rendering the germ cells largely independent of the somatic cells and their changes.

It is not only at this point, but at another also, that eugenics must receive help from modern biological knowledge. Without pledging ourselves to any special physiological theory of heredity, it is quite possible to investigate the facts of heredity and to measure the rate of inheritance of any character in man living in a community. If we accept the theory of Mendel we reach in broad lines the same theoretical results as the Biometric School has reached from dealing solely with the statistics of populations, namely, there is an average degree of resemblance between parent and child, and this degree is lessened in geometrical progression as we pass to grandparents and great-grandparents. Now as eugenists our object is to determine to what extent a differentiated class of the community impresses its characters on its offspring, and the average effect is what we are seeking. It is not needful to pledge ourselves to any one theory of inheritance. What we want to ascertain are the proportions of children who will be born able in able stocks and in dull stocks ; what are the proportion of children who will develop insanity in sound and in unsound stocks. The exact mechanism by which these proportions are maintained is of vital interest to science, it is not essential when we have to deal with mankind in the mass and prescribe social treatment for differentiated classes.

In later lectures you will be shown how these problems of inheritance have been approached from the statistical standpoint. It will be indicated to you that with our present knowledge we can safely affirm that not only physical but psychical characters, and not only psychical characters but morbid and pathological constitutions, are largely, and probably in absolutely equal degree, the product of inheritance. Indeed were we the ' superman ' we could breed a race of abnormally shy men, as we could breed a race of abnormally tall men , and we could breed a race in which six fingers were the rule or one in which nearly every member was a deaf-mute.

To sum up, then, this preliminary statement of what eugenists may claim as bricks for the foundations of our new structure :—

(1) We depart from the old sociology, in that we desert verbal discussion for statistical facts.

(2) We apply the new methods of statistics which form practically a new calculus.

(3) We start from three fundamental biological ideas —

(a) That the relative weight of nature and nurture must not a priori be assumed but must be scientifically measured ; and thus far our experience is that nature dominates nurture, and that inheritance is more vital than environment.

2—2

(*b*) That there exists no demonstrable inheritance of acquired characters Environment modifies the bodily characters of the existing generation, but does not modify the germ plasms from which the next generation springs. At most environment can induce a selection of germ plasms among the many provided determining which shall be potential and which shall remain latent.

(*c*) That all human qualities are inherited in a marked and probably equal degree.

If these ideas represent the substantial truth, you will see how the whole function of the eugenist is theoretically simplified. He cannot hope by nurture and by education to create new germinal types. He can only hope by selective environment to obtain the types most conducive to racial welfare and to national progress. If we see this point clearly and grasp it to the full, what a flood of light it sheds on half the schemes for the amelioration of the people, and half the projects of unthinking charity ! The widely prevalent notion that bettered environment and improved education mean a *progressive* evolution of humanity is found to be without any satisfactory scientific basis. Improved conditions of life mean better health for the existing population , greater educational facilities mean greater capacity for finding and using existing ability; they do not connote that the next generation will be either physically or mentally better than its parents. Selection of parentage is the sole effective process known to science by which a race can continuously progress The rise and fall of nations are in truth summed up in the maintenance or cessation of that process of selection. Where the battle is to the capable and the thrifty, where the dull and idle have no chance to propagate their kind, there the nation will progress, even if the land be sterile, the environment unfriendly and educational facilities small. Give educational facilities to all, limit the hours of labour to eight-a-day—providing leisure to watch two football matches a week—give a minimum wage with free medical advice, and yet you will find that the unemployables, the degenerates and the physical and mental weaklings increase rather than decrease. Then when your society is on the down-grade, you will perceive that in granting what each democracy must demand and what each individual claims as a social right, you have made the grant in such a way that the old safeguard for national welfare, the selection of parentage, has been sacrificed, and that it has to be laboriously re-established by new social sanctions. If these fail, then the collapse of your civilisation follows, and it will be replaced by a barbarism which pays little heed to or even rejoices in the cruelties of uncontrolled natural selection. Loaves and the circus—wages for the unemployable and the public football match to kill time—are as much signs now as of old that selection is being suspended, and that suspension undoubtedly means the rapid multiplication of the unfit at the expense of the fit.

The man in the street looks upon society and the nation as a very stable structure, which continues from generation to generation to exhibit the like social habits and the like marked racial features.

But is this really a correct view? I must confess that when I approach any class of the nation and statistically study it through two generations I fail to find this supposed stability. Mentally and physically each stratum of the community appears to be ever in flux. Nor I think are the reasons for this change far to seek. They will be found in the two demonstrable facts :—

(i) That a selective death-rate is always at work in human societies ; and,

(ii) That the rate of reproduction of the various sections of any community is widely different.

Man is a slow-thinking animal : he takes a long time to grasp a new idea, and a still longer time to let it take its place in the atmosphere of associations, which is the medium through which he views his own relations to the universe, and discriminates the social and the anti-social in conduct. It is now fifty years since the *Origin of Species* was published. We can now determine, and we have determined, the measure of the selective death-rate in man. Death is not a random archer, as he was thought to be of old. In from 50 to 75 per cent. of cases the bolt of death is not random, but seeks the weak joint in the armour, the constitutional defect, the predisposition, which we know in many cases to be an inheritance. To the individual and his immediate friends death and the crippling of activity by sickness and disease appear as the harshest contrasts of natural law and human hope and sympathy. So great is, and must be, the personal feeling in this matter, that in fifty years we have scarcely risen to the conception that death in its chief form—the selective death-rate—is the principal factor which maintains and elevates racial fitness ; that the great function of eliminating the weeds is maintained in the garden of human life by the hand of death. • Individually we shall never, perhaps, be able to realise in this wastage of life the hand of a beneficent gardener. But for those who would endeavour to study human life from the outside, and judge what tends to improve or to impair its efficiency, the selective death-rate must remain a great and racially beneficent factor. There are two lines which often ring in my ears, and which presumptuously I would have had the poet express somewhat otherwise :—

So careful of the type she seems,
So careless of the single life.

The welfare of the type is the outcome not of the careless, but of the heedful destruction of the single life.

It is not the repression of human emotions, but the examination of life from a different—I will not venture to say higher—aspect which leads some of us to-day to question whether the many social changes which soften life to the individual, which lessen the selective death-rate, tend to the final welfare of humanity. The conception of the destruction of the less fit as a beneficent factor of human growth must become part of our mental atmosphere, we must look upon it as a chief cause of the mental and physical growth of mankind in the past, not as a blind and hostile natural force carelessly crushing the single life, but as the source of all that we value in the intellect and physique of the highest type of mankind to-day.

The time may come when human society can undertake for itself what natural selection has wrought for it in the past ; but the suspension of the selective death-rate must go step by step with reforms which shall consciously replace the vigorous effectiveness of the old system. Therein lies the purport of eugenics. For how does Nature work through the selective death-rate ? Simply and effectively. By the death of those who cannot stand the strain of life, she removes the weaker stock before it has had any, or its full quotum, of offspring. When man knows better than at present which are the qualities which fit him for his task and for his environment, he may consciously undertake what Nature has done for him by her selective death-rate; to prepare him for this function is the true aim of the science of eugenics. But when the eugenist realises the difficulties in his way, when he comes in the future to sum up his success and his failure, I fancy he will turn with a feeling akin to gratitude to that blind force of Nature—the selective death-rate—which led man in his younger days irresistibly along the path of progress.   There are religious faiths which look upon pain as a divinely administered good—as a beneficial discipline.   May not something of the same kind be realised by those who stand on the firm platform of evolutionary science in the fiftieth year of its life?   Death, not the random archer of mediæval notion, but the skilful marksman whose aim is planned, has been in the past, and may perhaps long continue to be, the chief source of human progress as a whole. On the martyrdom of men is built the triumph of mankind

I have wandered somewhat from my point—the unstable character of human society owing to the selective death-rate —but I would impress upon you the fact that unless the eugenist realises the vastness of the forces at present at work moulding human life, he cannot hope to take definite action—an action based upon firm knowledge—when he comes to the criticism of present social tendencies.

The eugenist as far as lies in his power has to replace the selective death-rate by a selective birth-rate.   The past has depended for progress on *Natural Selection,* can the future depend for progress on *Reproductive Selection*?   My aim to-day is to insist on the gigantic part these two forces play in the evolution of human communities.

You may not unreasonably say that I have so far talked much about the selective death-rate but given you no proof that natural selection really plays a part in human develop-ment   I gave the proof many years ago as a modest reply to Lord Salisbury's famous Oxford address asserting that nobody had seen Natural Selection at work.   Of course no biologist paid any attention to my proof at the time, and it remained the special knowledge of biometricians, until Professor Ploetz of Munich turned it up recently (1909) and reasserted its correctness.

THE GROUNDWORK OF EUGENICS

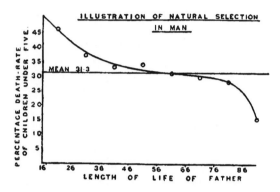

Fig. 1

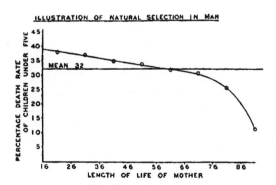

Fig. 2

PLATE II

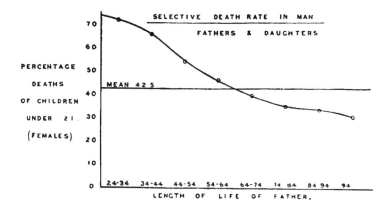

Fig 3

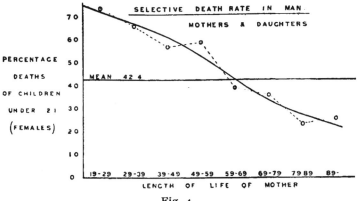

Fig. 4

The measure of the selective death-rate is extraordinarily simple. It consists in the fact that the inheritance of the length of life between parent and offspring is found statistically to be about one-third of the average inheritance of physical characters in man. This can only be due to the fact that the death of parent or of offspring in a certain number of cases is due to random and not to constitutional causes.

Let p be the chance of death from a random, not a constitutional source, then $1 - p$ is the chance of a selective death in parent and $1 - p$ again of a selective death in the case of an offspring, then[1]

$(1 - p)^2$ must equal about $\frac{1}{3} = \cdot36$ more exactly

$\therefore 1 - p = \cdot6$

and $p = \cdot40$. In other words 60 per cent. of deaths *are selective.* I put this result—tested from many series—quite broadly, and concluded that 50 to 75 per cent. of deaths in man were due to Natural Selection. I can bring this fact home to you by Figs. 3 and 4 of Plate II. It is the same matter looked at from another light. You will note the steady decrease of the death-rate with the greater constitutional strength of the parents.

In Table I, I have taken female children up to twenty-one, *i.e.,* practically those that die before reproduction You will see that whenever constitutional defect involving early death occurs in the parent, the children die at the appalling rate of more than 70 per cent before twenty-one. If the parent be long-lived, then only 30 per cent. die early. My data are from well-to-do Quaker stocks, and this death rate is thus not the result of absence of care or of means of livelihood. Professor Ploetz, who suggested this method of examining the data, shows the same thing in two series

[1] *Phil. Trans*, vol. 192A p 277 ; *Biometrika,* vol. 1 p 74.

of his own, one of middle-class and the other of Royal families (where no neglect can be supposed)[1]. His

TABLE I. INFLUENCE OF PHYSICAL CONSTITUTION OF PARENTS ON THE DEATH-RATE OF THEIR OFFSPRING.

A. MOTHERS AND DAUGHTERS.

Age of Mother at Death

Offspring	19-29	29-39	39-49	49-59	59-69	69-79	79-89	89 and over	Totals
Died before 21	36	122	123	111	115	162	91	22	782
Survived 21 ..	13	63	93	77	180	291	283	64	1064
Totals ...	49	185	216	188	295	453	374	86	1846
Death-rate	73·5	65·9	56 9	59 0	39 0	35·8	24 3	25 6	42 4

B. FATHERS AND DAUGHTERS.

Age of Father at Death.

Offspring	24-34	34-44	44-54	54-64	64-74	74-84	84 94	94 and over	Totals
Died before 21	34	83	118	144	202	194	71	7	853
Survived 21 ...	13	43	100	168	309	365	142	16	1156
Totals ...	47	126	218	312	511	559	213	23	2009
Death-rate	72 3	65 9	54 1	46 2	39·5	34 7	33 3	30 4	42·5

In these Tables 19–29 means all ages greater than 19 and less than 29 years.

[1] See *Archiv fur Rassen- u. Gesellschafts-Biologie*, Bd. VI. S. 33, 1909.

results are shown in Figs. 1 and 2 of Plate II. He takes only the infantile mortality (under five years), and he concludes that 60 per cent. at least of deaths are purely selective. Such is the demonstration of the enormous part which has been played by Natural Selection in man. Fifty years after the publication of the *Origin of Species*, it is purely idle to discuss, as our leading journal recently did, whether Natural Selection has or has not application to man. It has been demonstrably a really gigantic factor of continuous change in human societies.

If I turn to my second factor of social instability—the differential birth-rate—I must strive to convince you that reproductive selection is only second to natural selection in its vast reaching effects on human life. If society is to reproduce itself without change from generation to generation, then, accepting the inheritance of human characters, each subclass of the community endowed with its special grade of intelligence or physique must be equally fertile. If it is *not*, then the successive generations will not be identical, and can only be made identical owing to a selective death-rate.

There are few persons who realise on how relatively small a portion of each population the next generation depends. We have first to consider that many never reach the reproductive age at all. Here is the chief harvest of the selective death-rate. In England of 1000 males born only 680 live to be twenty, and of 1000 women only 708. Out of these adults we have next to estimate how many never marry or die without offspring. Here is the field not only of the selective death-rate, but of the selective marriage-rate. It is very difficult from any English statistics to determine how many adults never marry. No information on this point is asked in the death schedule for males ; it is asked, but imperfectly answered, in the case of the schedule for females. From statistics of other countries[1], it seems to me that about another 20 per cent. to 30 per cent. of adults never marry. To be on the safe side let us say that 50 to 60 per cent. of those born leave no offspring. Lastly, among those who do marry, how are the offspring distributed? Clearly those who have large families are responsible for a relatively large proportion of the next generation. Fig. 5, Plate III, illustrates the distribution of size of completed families in Quaker stocks. You will notice at once that the mean family is about 4·2 children. On the other hand about half the families have less, half more, than 3·3 children. Let us call families with less than 3·3 children *subfertile* and those with more *superfertile*. Then let us ask what relative amount of offspring the 50 per cent. of subfertile and the 50 per cent. of superfertile parents produce. The dotted curve gives the answer; it represents in percentages the total number of children produced, and we find the 50 per cent. of subfertile parents only provide about 25 per cent. of the next generation whereas the superfertile parents give 75 per cent. This law is practically universal for mankind;

---

[1] One of the many grave defects of the English system of census and registration returns is the absence of any record of civil condition in the male death registration. The Registrar-General informs me that the record of civil condition in the case of female deaths is worthless, and that no useful return can be made from it. In the Argentine I find that 60 per cent. die unmarried. In the returns for 1861 and 1862 for Scotland, 39,318 females died unmarried out of 65,467 deaths, again almost exactly 60 per cent. Working on the last United States Census I find that 51 per cent. of the population died unmarried, and on the last two English Censuses and the *Annual Reports* that 48 per cent. died unmarried. This indirect method of reaching the result is, however, not very satisfactory. We may, I think, conclude in round numbers that 40 per cent. of the population dies before it reaches twenty-one (see Figs. 3 and 4) and that probably another 20 per cent. are never married.

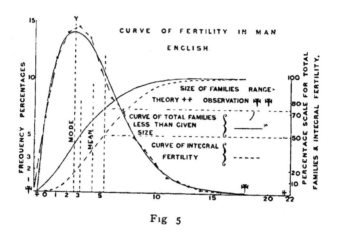

Fig 5

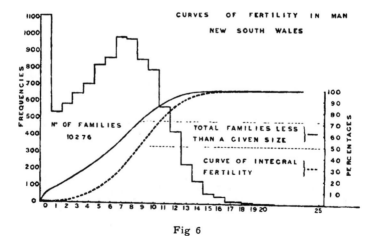

Fig 6

PLATE III

ILLUSTRATION OF EFFECT OF A RELATIONSHIP BETWEEN FERTILITY & INTELLIGENCE

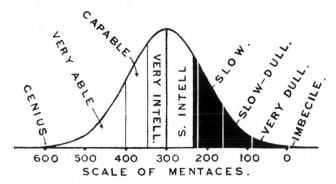

Fig. 7

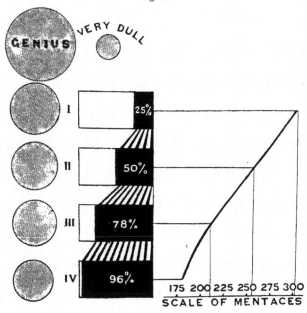

Fig. 8

it has been confirmed for Denmark and for New South Wales (Fig. 6, Plate III)[1]. Fifty per cent of the married population provide 75 per cent. of the next generation. The same rule may be expressed in another way: 50 per cent. of the next generation is produced by 25 per cent. of the married population, or about 12 per cent. of all the individuals born in the last generation provide half the

TABLE II. PROPORTION OF MATED INDIVIDUALS WHO PRODUCE 50 PER CENT. OF THE NEXT GENERATION

Species	Data	Percentage of Matings
Man ..	English (Pearson) ..	25
,, ...	Danish ,,	25
	New South Wales (Powys) .	
,, ...	Professional Classes -	23
,, ...	Domestic ,,	23
,, . .	Commercial ,, ...	23 }Mean 25
,, ...	Industrial ,, ..	25
,, ...	Pastoral ,, . .	27
Mice ..	Weldon ...	35
Poultry ..	Pearl	36
Swine ...	Rommel	39
Horse .	Pearson {Fecundity ...	41
	{Fertility ...	25

next generation. This is not only a general law, but it is practically true for each class in the community. This law of mine holds in a lessened degee for other forms of life, but it appears to reach its highest intensity in the case of man (Table II). And I believe that this is largely due to certain artificial features of his civilisation. At least the

[1] I am inclined to differ from Powys and consider that this diagram indicates much artificial sterility

case of the thoroughbred race horse, with its artificial
conditions, tends to confirm this view[1]. Be this as it may,
it is of vital importance for the eugenist to realise how
relatively small an element of human society is responsible
for the next generation[2].

I want to emphasise this still more emphatically. Let
us assume that the 25 per cent. superfertile element in the
population has a lower average intelligence than the subfertile 75 per cent. If you look at Fig. 7, Plate III, giving
the distribution of intelligence in the population, based upon
observations of about 4000 school-children and 1000
Cambridge graduates, you will see that 25 per cent cor-
responds to about the range of slow, dull and mentally
defective. I have taken 100 units of intelligence, which I
term mentaces, to correspond to the range of the intellects
which fall between the specially able and the average man.
Now if we assume that the imbecile has zero intelligence,
you will find that the average man has about 300 or perhaps
rather more mentaces, and if we define genius to be about
'the one man in a thousand' level of ability, the genius has
some 600 or 700 mentaces. Now if we divide our population at 25 per cent., the mean number of mentaces of this
rather slow and dull group is 173 and of the 75 per cent.
342, the average man having 300 mentaces. Now notice
what happens if the line between the superfertile and sub-

[1] Judged from fecundity—the births to opportunity—the horse takes
its place properly among mammals. Judged by gross fertility it comes
close to man

[2] Critics have asked what Biometry has done during the fifteen
years of its existence to justify its claims as an instrument of biological
inquiry. It may be pertinently replied, that to have demonstrated
that 12 per cent. of one generation in man produces 50 per cent.
of the next generation, and to have measured the intensity of natural
selection in man, would be quite sufficient claim, had it not done, as
it has done, much else.

fertile be that of intelligence. In the next generation there
will be 50 per cent. of lower and 50 per cent. of the higher
grade of intelligence, with an average for the whole community of 257 mentaces, a fall of 43 mentaces in the general
ability of the population; in the next stage the superfertile
increase to 78 per cent. of the population and the average
ability has fallen to 210 mentaces ; in the third generation
the superfertile element has risen to 98 per cent. of the
whole and the average intelligence has fallen to 180 mentaces. In Fig. 8, Plate III, this drop is represented by the
continual decrease in the areas of the circles, as the lower
intelligences with the higher fertility rapidly predominate.
You will note the progression from genius towards extreme
dullness. To impress this dwindling of a character owing
to reproductive selection on my readers, I will suppose as a
second illustration that cranial capacity is associated with
the subfertile group. Skull I to the right of Plate I
marks the average man and skulls II, III and IV the
degeneration which would follow in three generations. I do
not intend by this to assert that intelligence is proportional
to cranial capacity ; it is not. But I want to emphasise the
deterioration which must follow association between fertility
and inferiority in any racially valuable characteristic. Bear
those skulls in mind and you will not easily forget the rate of
degeneration which must follow any differentiation of the
intelligence or worth of the population into superfertile and
subfertile groups. What I have said here applies not only
to intelligence and cranial capacity but to every quality
which may be associated with a differentiated grade of
fertility.

I do not think anything can be more eugenicly impressive
than this principle that if fertility be correlated with any
character, the population must be unstable.

And now I want to make a somewhat remarkable admission. Not only in man but in other types of life, it is extremely hard to find any character whatever *which organically is markedly associated with fertility*. Nature seems to have effectually hindered living forms from undoing by reproductive selection her great achievements produced by natural selection. It will be obvious to you that if one class which died twice as fast as a second, yet produced three times as many offspring, the increased fertility would more than compensate for the selective death-rate. I do know characters which are *slightly* related to fertility in man—notably a character which I will term ' toughness of constitution '—and measurable by longevity—the husband and wife who live to eighty will have on the average before fifty years of age more children than the pair who only live to sixty-five. But in Nature as a whole there is little relation of fertility to any good or bad qualities of the individual.

Where, then, is the moral of my tale, if there be no organic correlation between fertility and intelligence ? The answer lies in emphasising the word *organic*. What Nature has avoided man has artificially produced. That is the kernel of the whole matter for the science of eugenics. Approach the problem as we will, the conclusion forced upon us is ever the same, the physically inferior, the mentally slow are not naturally more fertile than the stronger in body and mind, but they are in our community to-day the more fertile, and the process of deterioration I have exaggerated in that series of skulls *is* in progress. The moment we suspend the full vigour of natural selection, the moment we artificially correlate fertility with any defect of physique or intelligence, we start that downward movement. To check this movement I take to be the special function of practical eugenic action.

The correlation between fertility and unfitness will no

doubt be discussed more fully later in these lectures, but I should like to indicate how complex the problem is, and how very difficult it is to obtain the facts one desires to know from the manner in which returns are made in government statistical offices. One has to turn to the countries of the new world to get data which ought to be provided in this; and then the social conditions are so different that we have to allow for wide possibilities of divergence in our results

If we look upon society as an organic whole, we must assume that class distinctions are not entirely illusory, that certain families pursue definite occupations, because they have a more or less specialised aptitude for them In a rough sort of way we may safely assume that the industrial classes are not on the average as intelligent as the professional classes and that the distinction is not entirely one of education.

Now the points we have to bear in mind are the following: (i) the size of completed families; (ii) the child mortality; (iii) the relative marriage-rate, (iv) the relative adult death-rate for each class. Only when we know all these fully, shall we be quite certain as to how the different classes in a community are altering New South Wales[1] is one of the few countries where such data are effectively recorded, and Table III illustrates the nature of the successive allowances to be made The table refers to the size of families of the various social classes at death of one or other parent.

The order of fertility is pastoral, industrial, commercial, domestic and last professional, and although the percentage child deaths are different in the different classes, yet the net offspring or those that survive to fifteen are in the same class order, each industrial family has on an average half a child more surviving than the average professional family. So far the balance is still in favour of the industrial class.

---

[1] Data from Powys, *Biometrika*, vol. IV. p. 233.

But the next column shows you that this is not the whole gain. The industrial classes are marrying at a far more rapid rate than any other class; five industrial marriages take place for every four professional marriages and roughly for

TABLE III. FERTILITY WEIGHTS OF VARIOUS
SOCIAL CLASSES.

COMPLETED FAMILIES. NEW SOUTH WALES.

Class	Gross Offspring	Percentage Deaths to 15	Net Offspring	Marriage-Rate	Death-Rate over 20	Fertility Weight
Pastoral	6·1	21 3	4·8	18 2	12 7	·82
Industrial .	5·2	27·0	3·8	40·5	22·7	1·28
Commercial ...	4 7	25·5	3·5	30 0	13·3	·98
Domestic ...	4·6	26·1	3·4	15·7	16 6	·48
Professional ...	4·4	25 0	3·3	32·8	15 7	·98
Whole population	5·4	24·1	4·0	27·8	16·5	1·00

COMPLETED FAMILIES. DENMARK.

Class	Gross Offspring	Percentage Deaths to 15	Net Offspring	Marriage-Rate	Death-Rate over 20	Fertility Weight
Pastoral ...	—	—	—	24·0	—	—
Industrial ..	5·3	40	3 2	24·8	26·9	81
Commercial ..	4 9	37	3·1	24·4	16·1	1·29
Domestic ...	6·5	28	4·7	—	—	—
Professional	4·8	29	3·4	15 9	15 1	·98
Whole population	5·0	36	3·2	22·6	19·8	1

every two pastoral marriages. These rates are not true for Europe. Westergaard and Rubin believe the marriage-rate of the professional classes in Denmark to be one-third less than that of the industrial classes. In our own country I doubt whether the professional marriage-rate exceeds half that of the industrial classes. Again, the small marriage-rate of the pastoral classes would only apply to a country where the agriculturist is largely a pioneer. So far, however, the race is markedly in favour of the industrial as compared to the professional group But here a new feature comes in—the industrial classes may need a larger increase, because their wastage is greater. In the next column I have placed the death-rates for the several classes, considering only adults over twenty. We find the death-rate is *selective*, but it by no means compensates for the greater marriage-rate and greater net birth-rate. In the last column I have allowed for marriage and death-rates of the various classes, and obtained what I term the fertility weight of the different classes The lesson to be learnt from this last column is twofold : (1) that society is not a stable whole, the different social classes multiply at very different rates, and (ii) that society recruits itself from below, the rate of reproduction of the industrial classes being 30 per cent. greater than that of the professional classes

We cannot apply these results directly to the state of affairs in England The marriage-rate of the professional classes is much lower, and of the pastoral classes higher ; the relatively low rate of those in domestic employment is of course maintained, but the inadequate multiplication of the domestic class is met by recruits, perhaps, as much from the pastoral as from the industrial classes. My object, however, is not to draw conclusions as to social classes, but to point out that our principle of treatment must be the same, whether we deal with social classes, intellectual grades, or mentally or physically defective groups. We have in each case to investigate their fertility weight as compared with that of other types. The aim of the eugenist is to enforce the principle, that society in every case must recruit itself ' from above,' where ' above ' has now to be interpreted not as referring to a social class level, but to the group with the higher grade of the nationally desirable characteristic.

Thus far we have seen the large part played by selective death-rates, selective birth-rates and selective marriage-rates in determining the nature of the community, and in this you may have realised how the science of eugenics is really embraced in the statistical or actuarial study of the growth of human society But a study of death and fertility would carry us but little way, had we not some measure of how the parental characters of each differentiated group are handed down to their offspring. The results I am going to try and impress upon you in conclusion to-day are based upon the measurement of more than 1000 families, and, as will be shown you in later lectures, may be considered closely true not only for physical, not only for pathological, but for mental characters.

Men and women do not mate at random ; our measurements and observations show that for practically all characters there is a selective mating, like tends in a sensible but small degree to mate with like. Assuming this 'assortative mating' to exist, let us term exceptional the man or woman who possesses more of a given character than every nineteen persons out of twenty. Thus the tallest man in a *random* twenty shall be called exceptionally tall ; the best in a random class of twenty students exceptionally intelligent. This is nothing more than a definition of what we will call for the time being 'exceptional.' Now I found from our study of the inheritance of human characters that fifty-two marriages in 10,000 are of an exceptional man and woman, 9948 are of pairs of which neither or only one are exceptional. In the fifty-two exceptional marriages, exceptional children are produced in the ratio of nearly 26 exceptional to 26 unexceptional, or about half the children are excep-

THE GROUNDWORK OF EUGENICS

PLATE IV

tional. Of the 9948 unexceptional pairs, the ratio will be 474 exceptional to 9474 unexceptional children, or rather less than one-twentieth of the children will be exceptional.

Thus while eighteen times as many exceptional children will be born of commonplace as of exceptional parents, the commonplace pairs only produce exceptional children at one-tenth of the rate of the exceptional parents. That great men are usually born of commonplace parents is only a paradox, when we forget that commonplace pairs of parents are 200 times as frequent as pairs of exceptional parents, and that accordingly the small chance of an exceptional son occurring to any commonplace pair is made up for by the far greater number of such pairs.

The model photographed in Plate IV is an endeavour to illustrate the point on which after all most eugenic inquiries must turn. In the relatively small cube in the corner is a profusion of individuals represented by black peas bearing the character you want for national purposes. In the great mass of the general population represented by the remainder of the cube you see the sparsity of persons gifted with this advantageous character. The bulk do not possess it, or perhaps possess its opposite, a detrimental attribute. Even in the general population the majority of these scattered black peas would be found concentrated round the exceptional corner.

Now let us fully grasp this—a minority in the community producing the coloured or desirable in profusion, a majority producing the desirable very sparsely, and the colourless or undesirable profusely. Grasp further that social and political measures have reduced and will continue to reduce the stringency of the selective death-rate between these two classes. In the present state of social feeling we have only one resource for remedying this—the selective birth-rate.

In the light of the recent work of Heron and others, can we definitely place our fingers on any desirable social characteristic to-day which has a selective birth-rate in its favour?

I believe that there is not a single character which makes for national welfare, which can be shown definitely to be favoured by a selective birth-rate at the present time. Social conditions have allowed prepotent birth-rate to be associated with a tabid and wilted stock. It would matter little were not the same conditions suspending also the old selective death-rate. Combined, these two factors must give in the future the degeneracy I have endeavoured to illustrate to-night

These are the chief lessons which biological truths as applied to man have to teach us. Natural fertility is not markedly associated with good or bad characteristics. Given a high birth-rate and a heavy death-rate Nature will preserve and advance her human type with a cruelty to the individual, which social feeling is too strong at present to permit of, and political power too democratic to leave unchecked. But when the selective death-rate is reduced, as far as legislation, municipal hygiene, state support, medical progress and unlimited charity can reduce it, then what means are left by which mankind can consciously undertake the task which Nature has hitherto so ruthlessly carried out?

With the advance of civilisation the birth-rate as well as the death-rate has become more and more artificial. But it has become artificial in an individualistic and anti-social way. The purport of eugenics is to study the causes of this change, to create a strong public opinion, a new moral sense on this cardinal factor of national welfare. A progressive and imperial nation can only afford to be kind to its weak in body or mind if that kindness synchronises with the determination that each successive generation shall be better born. We have to take social customs as we find them. We must recognise to the full that human fertility changes in highly civilised states from the natural to the artificial phase. Such change led, in my opinion, to the collapse of the great civilisations of the ancient world. It will lead to the downfall of the great civilisations of to-day, unless our clearer scientific insight enables us to recognise, our more intense social spirit leads us to stem in time, the ills which inevitably flow from the suspension of the selective death-rate, and the artificial creation of a cacogenic selective birth-rate.

It is a hundred years since Charles Darwin was born, fifty years since he turned the search-light of natural selection on the then dark mystery of living forms. It is fitting that this anniversary year should proclaim that the knowledge thus gained has a great practical application to the welfare of human societies. The coping-stone is not of necessity the most structurally important block in every building. Yet in asserting that the science of eugenics forms the coping-stone to the science of life, we shall emphasise that the highest function of science is to be of direct practical service to man, the lower functions are to discipline and train his mind, to occupy and interest his leisure. The fitness of eugenics as an academic branch of study lies not alone in the training it requires, which carries us at the same time into the new world of biological conceptions and into the older world of accurate quantitative analysis. It lies also in the groundwork it supplies for the treatment of those great social problems, on the adequate and expeditious solution of which lies, in the opinion of the more thoughtful men and women of to-day, the main, if not the sole, safeguard for future national progress.

CAMBRIDGE PRINTED BY JOHN CLAY, M A AT THE UNIVERSITY PRESS